My Memory of Poetry

My Memory of Poetry

MICHELLE LYN COLLINS

ISBN: 978-1-64921-229-0   (Paperback Edition)
ISBN: 978-1-64921-230-6   (Hardcover Edition)
ISBN: 978-1-64921-228-3   (E-book Edition)

Some characters and events in this book are fictitious. Any similarity to real persons, living or dead, is coincidental and not intended by the author.

Book Ordering Information

Phone Number: 347-901-4929 or 347-901-4920
Email: info@globalsummithouse.com
Global Summit House
www.globalsummithouse.com

Printed in the United States of America

She has the best family. She grew up in West Virginia and has a twin brother. But when she was 38 yrs old, her sister put her to a mental hospital because they say she was mentally ill for having anorexia. She was told by the minister that she doesn't have a mental disorder, but God sometimes makes some situations in order to meet people that you need. Everything happens for a reason.

Wants to dedicate with friends and family.

Nice on over WVU line never had a life for few years

Then went a mile passed Pennsylvania line

All that wining said never want ever be WVU women

I'm not lying

Missed my counselors an missed shot had too much about it
just too many

Spazem or be breeze bout it

Roses are red violets are blue

Sugar is sweet and so are you

Such a shame I'm not the blame

But could never be you down like you

Black and yellow just made million

Have another schedule you know

What it is its free compared something

Chestnut ridge had a horror film

All the pretty bells and freshly smells

Really if i fell

At least I got my mail and felt like dumbbell

Ol better then hell

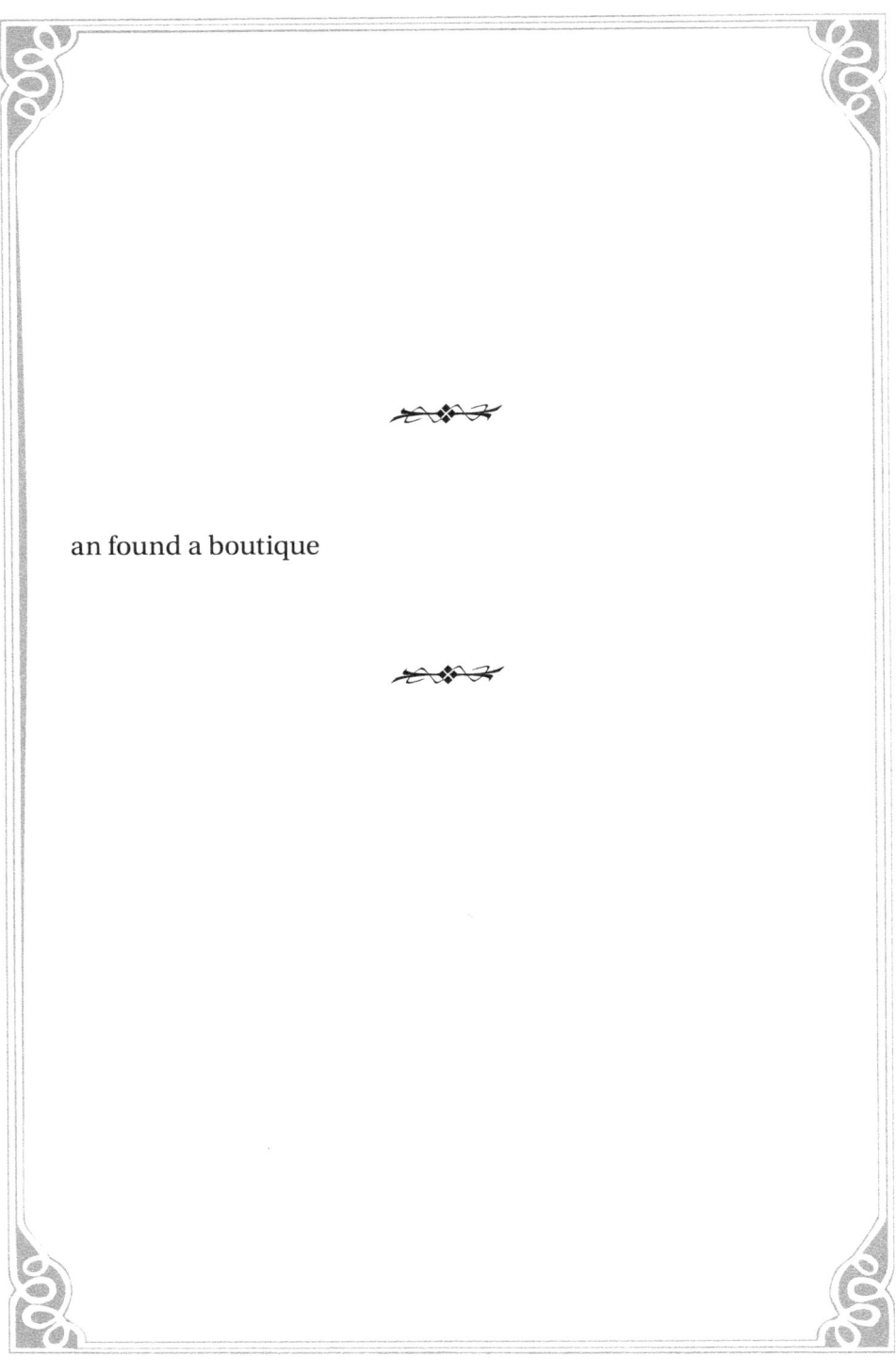

an found a boutique

Cafe le petite something to eat

A little something to eat

How sweet cafe le petit

Hot to trot

But though that's not would a tied

Tied the knot

And dropped it why not

Crystal blue lake really is fake

Make my tummy ache

When i drank an really shake n bake

Happy St. Pattys day hip hip hoorah

Green is the scene

But don't get mean

Have fun and shake your bun

So go find your one

Get ready for fun

Blue moon where you from

And come near and far

It's that fair

Not even blue tear

Roses are red violets blue

If ya hear another rhyme

Might suck for you

My twin even too cool

Miss my tee pee

Just my green eyes

You can see lucky me

Even with my green tea

Poor pitiful even me

Himalayan mountains falling water

From icy blue fountain

Why be at country mountain

Wining bout really nothing bout em

Chai tea shortly all about me

How sweet can that be all mean mama

Hey no more damn drama

Had my pina colata so how's Obamas

Cherry blossom just seen posem

Must be dream had awesome

Even Japanese blossom must a moved an been forgotten ol

Well afterlife might be awesome

Should a flew in ashoot

Pirates riots parrots a lot cool boots hoots for a flute

Too cute and a mute

Hollywood all good we could be down in hood hollywood

doing well you know glad they could

Mountaineers were pioneer

How it feels were really here free

It's wonderful to be mountaineer

No matter what some to blame who's here

Everyone get wedding day degree

I get for free for me

Wonderful as can be god gifted

Yay to me just really wasn't meant to be

Had spot a tea an jewelry party a lot english said

Never heard of so much about it but you

Mountaineers are tough more then even men real

World really would punch em out about it what

Have nerve for all the gossip they do about it

Stole my West Virginia from me Pennsylvania

Almost had it some rough in then breezy even

Spazem turn right about it missed a even shot

Could a been better about it fatty liver an about

Fell over dead hows million really deserve more about it

Even if Jesus is near know that wasn't for him

I wouldn't be here said all innocent blame for

No reason here I'll be there bruise my wrist

Get sharps out of there

Thanks to green county thinking clear how can

Some of make it threw too much i have my

Crystal ball right here my mountaineer land

Threw me over here

Kelly and I angel fell from sky were two of

Kind had mean mission about died bad to take

Someone's life invite even reply

Prettier and greener on across side at and

Still no place like across Pennsylvania

Roses are red violets are blue about had

Me with my wedding my farm even my dog too

Jesus even appeared knew we were here a angels really care

Why be upset superwomen here

Who really even cares

It's real fair

Need mental hospital derserves pepperspray even police say
yeah for me an her we shoot em for sure

CPSIA information can be obtained
at www.ICGtesting.com
Printed in the USA
BVHW070934081220
594972BV00001B/118